Downhill Techniques
for
Off-Road Runners

By

Keven Shevels

TRAIL GUIDES
publications

First published in Great Britain in 2005 by Trailguides Limited.
Second edition published In Great Britain in 2010 by Trailguides Limited.
www.trailguides.co.uk

ISBN 978-1-905444-38-0

Trailguides Limited
35 Carmel Road South
Darlington
Co Durham DL3 8DQ

Cover design by Steve Gustard.

Contents

1. Introduction

Ok, so you're an off-road runner. It doesn't matter whether you orienteer, run on the fells or run on the trails, you may even be one of those well-adjusted people who do all three. What does matter is that in nearly all off-road events there is a stage where you will end up running to the top of a hill. At this point the thought about coming back down will cross your mind. Anyway you run back down the hill and get to the bottom. You didn't do too badly, but you didn't do that well either. But after all, good downhill runners are born aren't they.

Wrong !

Anybody can become a better downhill runner. All it needs is a little knowledge, a bit of practice but more importantly the willingness to see that you can improve and the wish to do something about it. The practice and the willingness are your contribution. The knowledge is in this guide. Put them together and watch your downhills improve.

2. Physical Aspects of Running Downhill

2.1 What happens when you run downhill

We all know that when we run a hilly course, the next day the legs can ache something terrible. The blame for this is normally placed on the effort put in to climb the hills. In reality, it is the effort of coming down that causes the problems. So what is it about running downhill that is so stressful.

Well first off, muscle soreness most often happens when the muscle has to do a greater number of eccentric actions than it is used to performing. These eccentric actions are where the muscle tries to shorten while at the same time another movement is lengthening it.

When running, gravity pulls the knee downward on every foot strike. This is known as knee flexion. At the same time, one of the purposes of the quadriceps (quads) muscles is to shorten in order to prevent excessive knee flexion. So you have the situation where gravity and impact induced flexing at the knee stretches the quads at the same moment that they are being shortened to reduce knee flexion. This gives repetitive high-tension strain on each foot strike, which can be upto 80/90 times per minute on each leg. This is a considerable amount of, cumulative stress, which can result in significant muscle damage to the quads.

This is the situation in all running activities and normal training does tend to protect the quads as they just get used to a certain level of eccentric actions and stress.

However, running downhill multiplies the eccentric pulling apart stress on the quads as, because of the angle of descent, the leg falls a little bit further than normal on each stride. This increases the acceleration of the leg at the foot strike resulting in the forces that produce knee flexion being very much higher.

The quads are still performing their task of reducing knee flexion but because of the increased forces of the knee flexion, the stress that they have to cope with is very much greater. As a result, microscopic tears in the muscle fibres and connective tissues of the quad can happen. The end result is considerable soreness.

With the correct training and conditioning the body can be taught how to better control and distribute the forces that act on particular muscles. This will lessen the strain on each of the individual muscles as the eccentric actions try to tear them apart. In turn this will reduce the incidence of muscle damage and the resulting pain and soreness.

Conditioning the body to be more able to cope with this stress is the subject of the next section of this manual.

In addition to the physical stress of running down hill, there is also the mental stress of performing an activity that may not be considered "natural". This is dealt with in section 3 Mental Attitude.

2.2 Conditioning the body for downhill running.

As we have seen in the previous section, running downhill can be very stressful on the body. To enable the best performance the body needs to be conditioned to cope with this stress.

The most obvious way of conditioning the body to cope with running downhill is to actually run downhill. Regular downhill sessions will improve the body's ability to handle the stress loads. However, in addition to this there are two areas where the body can be given specific exercises. These two aspects of conditioning are strength and suppleness.

1. Strengthening exercises can be used to increase specific eccentric strength. If the muscle is stronger then it's ability to handle the relevant stress will be increased thus reducing the chances of injury. It will also increase the endurance capacity of the muscle so that it can cope with the stress caused by downhill running for longer periods before tiredness sets in.

2. Suppleness is about increasing the flexibility of a muscle. The shorter and tighter a muscle is, the more it is prone to tears and strains when it is asked to lengthen during exercise. Increasing the flexibility will improve your performance by allowing the muscle to be more adaptable and also reduce the chances of being injured.

We'll now look at these two areas in more detail.

2.2.1 Strength

All off-road runners need strong legs. Regular running on hills either as part of your steady running or as reps will build up the necessary strength. However for those who don't have regular practical access to the hills or who want to increase the strength levels of their legs, then a regular strength training regime is essential.

The obvious need for leg strength applies also for downhill work. The usual use of free weights and weight machines to do exercises such as squats, hamstring curls, etc also apply. However what these exercises don't address is the strength needed for the eccentric contractions that are directly applicable to downhill running.

There are two ways of approaching this area and both have their place in a strength-training regime.

Weight Training

Firstly using weights. Normal weight-training exercises don't really tend to touch eccentric contraction. However there is one notable exercise involving the use of an inverted leg press machine which is very useful. However be aware that this is a specialist exercise and involves overloading the leg muscles and should only be attempted under the guidance of a qualified weight lifting/training coach. This exercise can totally trash the quads for a period of time and should be performed no more than once every three weeks and definitely not at all during the competitive phase of the years training.

Basically it involves loading the inverted leg press machine with slightly more weight than you can actually lift in one single rep. Spotters will than assist you to lift the leg press into position. Once comfortable, the spotters will let go of the weights and the total weight will than be supported by the lifter.

Obviously with the weight being more than the lifter can actually raise, there is no chance of the lifter keeping the weight aloft. The intention is for the lifter to perform a slow controlled descent back down to the resting position.

An inverted leg press machine can be used to develop eccentric strength.

This descent is the eccentric contraction and performing it under the influence of the weights will increase it's strength. After an adequate recovery, the action would be repeated.

If performed correctly this is a very stressful exercise for the lifter and not too many reps should be performed. Word of caution, if doing this exercise under the direction of a specialist weights coach at a gym, be careful of how many reps they have you complete. Weight lifters can and do follow regimes that involve totally trashing one set of muscles to the point of total exhaustion and becoming totally useless for a couple of days. In the meantime they will work a totally different set of muscles until the first have recovered sufficiently to resume training.

This is not your intention, even though you should never follow a session like this with a heavy days training. Don't be afraid to call a halt to the session if you feel that you have done sufficient.

Plyometrics

Another way of gaining strength is by the use of plyometrics. Plyometrics are basically exercises designed to increase your explosive strength through activities such as bounding, hopping and jumping. Don't scoff; they are one of the most effective strengthening exercises around.

Plyometrics are a core part of the training for any sprinter or jumper but are sadly often neglected by both endurance runners and coaches.

To keep it at its most simple, what plyometrics do is to increase the strength that is required to lift the body up after it has landed on the stride. Sprinters and jumpers use plyometrics to increase the height, length and power on the take-off phase of their movement. There is no reason why a modified plyometric session more geared towards endurance should not help a distance runner to develop the specific strength to maintain form especially in the later stages of an event when tiredness sets in. This is particularly relevant for downhills where the extra burden caused by the gravitational force of running downhill has to be overcome to lift the body up again on the take-off stage.

Plyometrics are an extremely effective way of increasing eccentric strength. However they are also very intensive and because of the exaggerated foot strike they also multiply the impact shock. Because of this they should always be performed in well-cushioned shoes and on a soft surface. A level grassy field is ideal and never ever on concrete or tarmac. Female athletes should always be cautious about performing plyometrics in the week before their menstrual cycle as at this time they may be more susceptible to shin splints and stress fractures.

Various plyometrics exercises can be used such as depth jumps etc. However, silly as this may sound, but running is a one legged activity meaning that at any point in time the full body weight is supported by only the one leg. Therefore any strengthening exercise using both legs together such as squats or depth jumps will not be as specific or as effective as a one-legged exercise, i.e. single-leg squats or hops. The most effective plyometric exercises are therefore those that exaggerate the downward impact and at the same time require an exaggerated response after the impact, a single leg at a time. Two exercises fill these criteria namely, hopping and bounding.

Bounding is simply an exaggerated running action. Push-off with the left foot and bring the leg forward with the knee bent and the thigh parallel to the ground. At the same time, reach forward with the right arm. As the left leg comes through, extend the right leg back and it is kept extended for the duration of the push-off. Hold the extended stride for a brief time before landing on the left foot. Repeat with the right leg. Make each stride long and try to cover as much distance as possible.

One of the most effective training sessions that I've ever done involved these two plus backwards sprinting in a highly effective anaerobic session. The session was based on a football pitch going width-ways across. The first leg was bounding across the width and once across sprinting back to the starting point with no recovery. The next was a single-leg hop, it didn't matter if it was the right or left leg as you changed over legs at the halfway point, again across the width followed by a sprint back to the starting point. Again with no recovery, the next and final leg was a back-

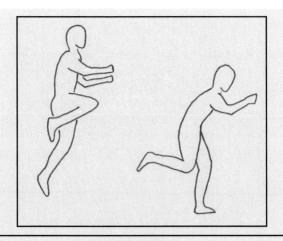

Single-leg hops.
Push-off with the leg that you are standing on and jump forward landing on the same leg. Immediately take-off again and repeat until the required distance is covered or number of hops is completed.
Try to cover as much distance as possible with each hop.

wards sprint across the width of the pitch with a sprint back again. That was the end of one rep. That would normally take around three minutes. Recovery would be 100% i.e. same time as the rep. Over time, I built up to do a set of five of these reps twice a week and had a series of my best race results ever, that is until I put my foot awkwardly on a stone and the whole lot came crashing down.

This is a very intensive session and not only is it a good strength builder but will also seriously build your anaerobic fitness. So two training sessions in one, how's that for economy of effort. I used this session to replace a weekly hill session during a period when I couldn't get into the hills on a regular basis and it really worked. However, because of it's intensity, never do this session in the week of competition.

Coupling weight-training and plyometric exercises
It is also possible to couple weight-training and plyometric work into the one exercise. This is known as complex training and can produce significant benefits in a short time.

A simple but effective exercise that is relevant to downhill running is to perform 10 single leg squats on the left leg and then straight away with no recovery, 10 left leg hops. Return to the starting position by repeating the process with the right leg.

Recovery for each leg would be while you were completing the process with the other leg. Slowly build-up to 10/12 reps with each leg. This exercise can be done as part of your warm-up routine, although not before a quality session, or as part of a circuit/strength session.

Bounding and hopping plyometric exercises can be used to develop height gained or distance covered. For the endurance athlete, it is probably better to focus on covering the greater distance for each bound/hop rather than trying to improve the height gained.

All exercises in this book either mobility, running or strength exercises should not be attempted without an adequate warm-up routine. Attempting any exercise "cold" before warming the muscles up sufficiently can lead to possible injury.

2.2.2 Suppleness

A regular general stretching routine or even a yoga session will provide enough flexibility to enable the body to cope with the demands of downhill running. However, there is one area that requires special focus and that is the groin area or to be more precise the adductor muscles.

The adductors are muscles that originate from the pubic bone on the inside of the thigh and run to the thighbone. They work quite powerfully as the foot leaves the ground and starts to swing forward. During the swing, the leg rotates outwards in relation to the hip. The adductors then come into play and swing the leg back towards the midline of the body.

Side stepping or a sudden change in direction while running, which often happens when running downhill on rough terrain, can over-exert these muscles and give considerable discomfort in the groin area, often called a groin strain.

This over-exertion is mainly caused by an inflexibility of these muscles. Incorporating specific exercises into your stretching routine will help act as a preventative against any possible injuries.

There are two simple exercises that are easy to perform and will greatly increase mobility in this area.

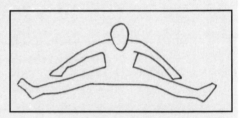

| Sit with the soles of the feet together. Use the hands to slowly press the knees down. You'll start to feel the stretch in the adductors. Hold for 30 seconds. Never push down with the hands to the point where it becomes painful. | Sit with your legs wide apart. Place your hands on the upper thigh. Slowly bend forward from the waist running your hands down the top of your legs. Feel the stretch and hold for 30 seconds. Again never perform to the point of pain. |

3. Technical Aspects of Running Downhill

3.1 Downhill techniques.

If running downhill were as easy as just putting one foot in front of the other such as in your local 10k then it would be a doddle. Unfortunately it isn't.

In this section, we will look at the various techniques that come into play when descending. There are a number of these factors that need to be considered in order to improve your downhill ability. Some of these will involve just sitting at home, others will involve getting out and running up and down the hills. However they all work. Give them a try and you will see improvement.

Stable and Unstable Ground

In this guide the terms stable and unstable ground are often mentioned.
In order to make the most effective use of his running stride the runner needs to place his/her foot on a hard level surface. This will enable them to make the most use of their energy and power to push themselves away from the ground on the take-off stage off the stride. The classic examples of a hard level running surface are athletics tracks and roads. These are considered to be stable surfaces.
In the off-road world nothing is as stable as these two although such surfaces as forest roads and well-made vehicle tracks can be considered as stable. Any other ground can be considered as being unstable to various degrees because it does not allow the runner to make the maximum use of his/her energy and power. This may be due to the ground being soft and absorbing energy or being uneven and/or loose and not allowing the runner to push-off in a straight line or it could be any combination of the two. Because of this, running on unstable ground is naturally slower than on stable ground.
All off-road running is classed as running on unstable ground. For the off-road runner, the choice is finding the least unstable ground to run over in order to make the most effective use of his/her running action.

3.1.1 Planning

It may sound silly planning your downhills but think about it and it becomes obvious. The only way to get the best out if yourself in any race is to plan your race and the downhills are a crucial part of that race.

In order to do this planning you need to know your race route. Know where both the uphills and where the downhills are, how steep are they and what is the terrain like. If you've done the race before then you'll probably know all this. If not, then you may have to do some research or at the least ask someone you know who has completed the race before.

However as part of the planning stage and as part of the preparation for a specific event there will be an advantage in actually running over the race route before the day of the event. This will give you the knowledge of the route in order to plan your race properly. In this way you can actually assess and choose your route and line of descent before the race begins.

This doesn't answer the question of why do you have to plan the downhills. The simple answer is that you want to complete the race in the shortest time possible and that does not necessarily mean that you should run flat out down the hill just because you can.

Some of the shorter races are straight up and down. Basically run up to the summit and then turn round and come back, with these races, there is the one descent and that goes to the finish line. In this case there is no argument about a flat out, eyeballs staring, hair- raising descent down to the tape.

However the more medium and longer length races are obviously longer in distance and do have more uphills and consequently more downhills.

The basic rule here is that the longer the race, the more that energy conservation becomes a factor. Granted running downhill takes less energy then running up but human nature being what it is, if you can run down a hill fairly quickly and you are passing other competitors at the same time, then you will do it. As has been said, downhill running takes less energy but it is deceptive in that it feels as if it takes less than it actually does.

When compared to running on the level running up an incline of 6% (6 metres of vertical climb per 100 metres of level distance) will use 35% more energy. On the other side running downhill on the same slope only reduces the effort by 24%. A mismatch of 9% of the runner's energy consumption. The popular misconception is that the descent will actually save you more energy than it actually does. Shows the importance of planning ....

It is a little bit pointless running hard down a hill if you find that at the bottom you've got to go straight back up another hill. This is where the planning comes in. Decide beforehand where on the course the effort is going to be put in and whether it is worth running hard downhill or would it be better taking it easier and saving energy for later on in the race. After all, it doesn't matter how fast you can run down a hill, what matters is how fast you can get round the whole course.

One other factor that needs to be considered when planning your race is risk assessment. After all, what we have said is that the important thing is to complete the course. If there is a particularly nasty descent halfway round the route do you decide to take it a bit easier to reduce the risk of falling resulting in injury and thus ensuring that you complete the race or do you go for it and accept the risk.

3.1.2 Route choice

Route choice is basically deciding which way to go. This can take two forms. With orienteering, mountain marathons and some fell races it is quite literally deciding which route to take. With some other fell races, trail races and cross-country the route is given i.e. the course is marked. In these cases the choice falls down to which side of the track to run on, where should I place myself for the descent etc. This is normally known as "taking a line". We will look at each of these in turn.

Route choice

For those events where there is an element of route choice, there are several factors that need to be taken into consideration most of which fall outside the scope of this manual. For those who want to look at this further, recommended reading is the sister publication "Mountain Marathon Preparation" and the Martin Bagness book "Navigation for Mountain Runners".

However, where there is a choice of descents to take, factors that come into play include :
1.   How long is the descent
2.   What is the nature of the ground underfoot
3.   How steep is the slope
4.   Are there any potential hazards if you go off route.

Taking a line

With taking a line, the basic rule is the shortest route is the quickest. The shortest route normally being a straight line.

However, there are other factors that need to be taken into account. These factors come down to the fact that in order to run fast you need a good solid surface for your running step to take-off from. Soft and unstable ground forces you to run slower. You therefore may have the case where if the straight-line route is over mud or a rough surface then avoiding the straight-line may allow you to run faster. Even though the distance is longer, the running time may be quicker.

Vegetation may also be a factor. High bracken, heather or even grass can slow you down considerably. If these are on your straight-line route then, again, the longer line round may be quicker.

3.1.3 Balance

When running downhill the most important thing is to get to the bottom in one piece and preferably still standing up. Therefore as you would expect a good sense of balance is important in maintaining an upright posture.

One of the main ways in maintaining balance is by using the arms as an aid. Tightrope walkers use them so why can't you. Raising the arms out from the side helps to maintain your balance. Try it and see.

Most off-road runners have a background in endurance running on roads or elsewhere. As endurance runners, one of the most fundamental aspects of running style and efficiency is the most energy efficient way of using the arms. The classic style for this is close to the side and moving backwards and forwards, slightly crossing the body. This leads to most runners having the mindset that this is the way you should use the arms and that you can't use the them any other way.

Forget the stereotype. If waving your arms about gets you safely to the bottom of the hill - then do it. It may not be totally energy efficient but there again, neither is lying in a crumpled heap at the bottom of the hill.

Using the outstretched arms to aid balance similar to a tightrope walker. A very effective technique for keeping the balance.

Exercises
There are various exercises in order to help develop your balance.

One that comes from the race walking fraternity is that of walking along a line with the feet going heel to toes. Very similar to the test to see whether you are drunk or not. As you walk, swing both arms round in wide circles. Sounds crazy but it works otherwise the race walkers wouldn't do it. This can be built-in to your warm-up routine either as part of a running session or a circuit training session.

Another example is using a wobble-board for a balance exercise. These are often used during rehabilitation from injury but can be used as a training aid in their own right. This also has the added benefit of strengthening the ankles.

If you don't fancy the expense of or don't

have access to a wobble-board, an alternative exercise is to stand on one leg with your arms out, slightly bend the knee and then close your eyes. Now try and stand like that for 30 seconds without falling over. Repeat a couple of times a day. Again, this also has the added benefit of strengthening the ankles.

And last but not least. Have a go at tight-rope walking, Set a rope up just above the ground or use a narrow plank of wood and walk along it. It's surprising how effective this can be in developing a sense of balance. Not surprising but this is an exercise often used by climbers.

As extra curriculum activities to running, any of the board sports such as skateboarding, surfing or snowboarding will all help to develop balance.

Never be afraid to use the arms to assist your balance.

3.1.4 Eye/foot co-ordination

All runners when they are descending a hill look where they are putting their feet. After all it is important to know what the foot is going to land on. However, the crucial thing here is where do you look ?

Think about it and I'll bet you say in front of the foot. But the question is how far in front of the foot ?

As they are descending most runners will watch the ground immediately in front of their feet to see what the foot is landing on. That is the problem. If you are looking at where the foot is landing you are in fact responding to what is already happening, you are not controlling your descent.

Where your eyes should really be focussing is three to eight paces in front of you. The eyes should be looking at the ground and assessing what you are going to be running over and not what you are currently running on. The brain will then have time to decide where the feet are going to and to pass the instructions that move them to the appropriate places.

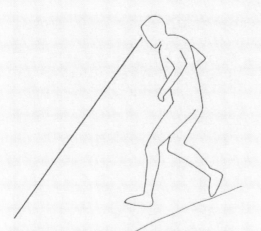

If running fast, you should be looking three to five paces in front. If travelling slower then five to eight paces.

Sounds simple but like a lot of things related to running downhill, it very rarely comes naturally. The common reaction to this principle is that "if I'm not looking at where my feet are going then I'm going to fall and get hurt".

Surprisingly enough if you look ahead and make a decision as to where you want your feet to go, then your body and its eye/foot co-ordination is normally bright enough to put your feet where you want with-

> Focus the eyes three to eight paces in front of you depending upon running speed. This gives you time to respond to changes in the ground in front and decide where your route choice is putting your feet. Once you have decided, the feet will automatically go there.

out you having to watch.

Exercises
This is a skill that most runners will definitely need to practice until it becomes automatic. The only way to do it is by live exercises descending a hill. This does not need to be done at race speed as once the ability is developed it will become automatic no matter what the speed of descent.

Focussing the eyes several steps in front to identify your foot placement.

3.1.5 Angle of lean

How can you control your descent speed?

One method is to obviously run faster or slower either by changing your stride length or changing your leg speed. Another method is using the angle of lean and adjusting the angle itself.

The angle of lean is the amount that the runner leans forward from the waist while running downhill. Using this angle of lean can help you control your speed without altering your stride length or leg turnover.

To gain momentum you can lean forward from the waist. This alters the runner's centre of gravity and increases forward speed. It does effectively put the runner slightly off balance and can give the impression of starting to fall down hill.

The problem with this technique is that the natural inclination while descending is to lean backwards. There is a natural aversion to leaning the body into a descent, self-preservation tells you not to make yourself so vulnerable.

Obviously runners come in all shapes and sizes and so it is difficult to say what is the best angle of lean for each individual runner. The centre of gravity will be different for each one dependant upon his or her own physical attributes, tall, short, big-chested, big-bellied etc etc. So what is required here is a little bit of experimentation on the part of the runner in trying this technique and seeing where their own choice lies.

The angle of lean can be changed to suit the angle of the hill. The shallower the hill the more the runner can lean forward. As the hill gets steeper, the closer to vertical the runner would get.

Leaning forward from the waist. The angle does not have to be significant, just one or two degrees from the vertical can increase momentum. Conversely, leaning backwards will slow momentum down.

Exercise.

Find a shallow hill with a grassy surface. Practice running down it and while doing it experiment with changing the angle with which you lean forward from the waist. As you run down lean forward and then lean back. See how your running speed alters without any change in your stride-length or leg-turnover. Practice and determine the angle with which you feel comfortable.

Experimenting with the angle of lean on a shallow hill.

3.1.6 Stride length.

When running downhill because of the angle of the slope and the assistance of gravity it is possible to take a longer stride-length than is normal when running on the flat. But is this effective?

The answer is yes and no.

The crucial factor for all downhill running is control. A longer stride-length means that when the foot hits the ground, the less the body weight is over the foot. This makes the foot strike unstable and means that it is difficult to respond to a bad foot plant or stepping on uneven ground.

Therefore the general rule is that the steeper the hill and the more unstable the underfoot conditions, the shorter the stride-length. The reverse also applies if the descent is shallow with a good running surface such as a forest road then it is possible to lengthen the stride to the point of over-striding.

However, as always keep your eyes open for hazards on the ground. Loose gravel is especially dangerous but there is also mud, ice, fallen leaves, bumps and holes in the ground and tree roots, just to mention a few. They are all slipping or tripping hazards and when encountered do necessitate reducing the stride-length.

> On shallower descents with a stable surface, running action can be maintained as normal and that includes stride-length.

One option to counter the slowing down effect of reducing stride-length is to develop a quicker leg turner. As speed follows the equation "Speed = Leg turnover x Stride-length", if you reduce stride length then increasing leg turnover will maintain speed.

Exercise
One painless way of helping to develop the ability to increase or decrease leg turn-

over for those with access to an exercise bike is to do a session with very low or nil resistance and keep a high leg revolution per minute. Over time this will crossover into your running and will accustom your legs to moving faster.

One other aspect of stride-length that relates to off-road running more than any other running discipline is the ability to change stride-length suddenly or even to leap over obstacles or hazards. This can happen when you are running on the level, uphill or downhill. At times there will be the sudden need to change stride-length for a couple of strides.

The ability to do these sudden changes can be hampered by an inflexibility or tightness in the adductor muscles. See the section on Suppleness.

Exercise
The only way to really develop the ability to stride-change quickly is by doing it. Pick a stretch of path between 100 metres to 200 metres in length that is quite rooty. The path should be on the level, this is more of a skill session so therefore the skill should be trained for in isolation rather than having to think about running downhill at the same time. Once developed the ability will cross over into your downhill running.

Slowly run the length of the path picking your way through the tree roots and then repeat. As confidence builds up so will the speed and the reaction time.

The last factor that can affect the choice of stride-length is the method of going downhill. There are two ways:

1.   Going straight down, and
2.   Contouring round and down.

While on steeper descents the stride-length will shorten.

Going straight down we've discussed above. Contouring down is where the runner follows the side of the hill effectively

24

following the contour lines as shown on a map (hence the name) while descending at the same time. With following the side of the hill the fact that one leg is usually slightly higher than the other inhibits stride-length. The technique here is to reduce stride-length while at the same time leaning the body into the hill.

Even on a supposedly "good" surface, erosion, weather conditions, other users or even forestry work can make the surface unstable. Always be prepared to alter your stride-length and running style if appropriate.

3.1.7 Foot plant

If trying to run downhill fast, it is very important to establish a sound foot plant. As you can imagine slipping or tripping is not really advisable due to the injury risk.

The best position for the foot is what is called the plantar flexed position. This is where the toes are pointing downwards so that the full sole of the shoe makes contact with the ground. This ensures the most effective use is made of the grip of the shoe sole whether it is studs, spikes or some variation of a waffle sole. On slippery surfaces such as wet grass or loose gravel this (full contact) may not guarantee staying upright but it gives you more chance than if you didn't.

On more shallow descents it is possible to maintain your normal foot plant whether it is toe first, heel first or whatever. Shallow descents give the opportunity to more follow your normal running pattern or style and that includes foot plant.

There is one exception to following the above and that is when descending a scree surface. Scree is loose stone ranging in size from little glass marbles to dinner plates. Standing on this with a flat foot is akin to standing on ball bearings, you never know which direction you are going to go in. The technique for descending this type of surface is the total opposite of the above. In this case the idea is to keep the body straight and land with the heels first and dig them into the scree whilst at the same time relaxing and letting the body slide a little so that the heels dig a little further in. For those familiar with winter hill walking it is much the same as coming down a snow slope and step kicking.

One aspect of running off-road particularly in rougher terrains such as encountered in some fell races is that you may not necessarily see where your foot is actually going to land. A particular case of this is when running through medium to high heather.

In these circumstances the runner has to learn to run with a "light foot". This means planting the foot and taking-off again without putting the full bodyweight on the

---

Often when running off-road, there will be an obstacle in the way such as a log, tree stump or large stone. One way of crossing these is to place the foot on the object and launch yourself over it. In these cases it is best to place the foot in the middle of the object with the bodyweight directly over the foot.

If the object is wet, slippery or even just rounded, placing the foot to either side of the middle point may result in the foot slipping sideways. At best this can lead to a loss of momentum, at worst it can lead to injury.

Descending where the view of the ground is obscured, in this case by bracken, practice will improve the ability and, even more importantly, the confidence to place the foot when you are not 100% certain of what is underfoot.

foot. If the foot does hit an obstacle such as a loose stone this will mean that the foot will not roll or turn so far as if the full bodyweight had landed. Obviously this will help reduce the chances of any injuries occurring.

This is not an easy skill to learn but with practice it can be developed.

Exercise
Pick a short section of level track about 200 metres long that is fairly rough but is completely visible. At a slow pace practice running along it trying not to put the full bodyweight behind the foot plant. Once you become familiar and accustomed to it a faster pace can be developed. When you feel comfortable with this then try running along a track where the vegetation obscures the path beneath your feet. Again, once you are confident with this move the exercise to a downhill stretch of track.

3.1.8 Stamina-lactic build up

One of the main problems that occur in races that have long downhills of two miles/ three kms or more is that of lactic tolerance. Lactic is a by- product of anaerobic effort and is the substance that builds up in your muscles. Once a high level is reached the leg muscles tire and slow down, sometimes quite dramatically.

Normally, the shorter the race distance, the faster you can run which creates more anaerobic effort and speeds up the lactate build-up. Running uphill adds to the problem, running up hill requires more energy and therefore more oxygen. As breathing and heart rate would be already close to their limit, the amount of extra oxygen available is small resulting in oxygen debt. More anaerobic energy is then used with the corresponding increase in lactate level.

So by the time you have got to the top of the hill there are already high levels of lactic in the leg muscles. This immediately puts you at a disadvantage on the downhill where there is a natural increase in pace just as the leg muscles are already beginning to tire and slow down.

There are two approaches to counter this:
1. Better pace judgment on the uphills
2. Improving lactic tolerance through training

Pace judgment

No doubt you'll have heard this many times before but in races that have several climbs, early pace judgment is essential.
A too fast start can totally ruin your race. Try to maintain a constant energy output as you run uphill even if it means slowing the pace.
In shorter up and down races, it is possible to maintain pace with relatively high levels of lactate in the muscles. However, judging how high this level can be before tipping you over the edge is not easy to estimate and, to be honest, comes with experience.

Improving lactic tolerance

Nearly all running books and magazines contain details on sessions designed to improve lactic tolerance. This is usually called threshold running, as the aim is raise the lactic tolerance or threshold. Normally they are all a variation on a continuous run for 20-30 minutes at around the 10k race pace or with the heart rate at 90% of maximum.

One session that I've used in the past and is more appropriate to downhill running, utilises a three and a quarter mile/five km steady uphill climb on dirt roads in my local forest. Steady run up to the top and then with no recovery so that the lactic levels are still quite high, turn around and do a pace run back down to the bottom. About three quarters of the way down the legs really start to feel it.

With this type of session it is best done on a smoother surface such as a forest dirt road or track. The emphasis is on maintaining pace and not practicing downhill technique so don't use a descent that is too rough or steep. This exercise can be done as a session in it's own right or, with correct planning, built into a long steady run.

Improve lactic tolerance by 20 to 30 minute steady paced runs at 10k race pace.

3.1.9 Transition

What is transition ?

Transition is that moment when the movement changes from one type to another.
With downhill running this can happen in three ways.
1.   The transition at the summit from running uphill to running down hill.
2.   The transition at the bottom of the hill from running down to running on the
        level.
3.   The transition at the bottom of the hill from running down to running uphill.

From uphill to downhill
In most off-road events be it trail, fell or xc, the moment will arise where you have
run powerfully up the hill and then reach the top and then start to come back down
again. At this point the majority of runners start to relax and actually treat the downhill as a recovery. This is mainly due to the sudden feeling of relative effortlessness
compared to the uphill, that is now experienced. The problem is that to maintain the
same speed less effort is required and so the runner tends to relax. Unfortunately this
tends to lose a possible advantage. Instead of maintaining the same speed for reduced effort, the effort level should be maintained, this will result in increased speed
just at the moment when competitors are relaxing. Very quickly a gap can be opened
up between you and your fellow runners by maintaining the effort up and over the
top of the hill even just for a short period. This is known as "running over the hill".

Exercise
Perform a series of hill reps where you can run up and over the top of the hill and
descend for 200/300 metres. Put the effort in running up and maintain it over the top
and down the 200/300 metres of descent.

From downhill to level
The sense of relative effortless running comes to an end when the bottom of the hill
is reached. All of a sudden the help that gravity gives when descending suddenly
vanishes and, instead the leg muscles have to start working hard again. This sudden
change can produce a touch of the old leg "wobbles "particularly if there is a change
in running surface, for example, from path to tarmac. Once again, the best way to
prepare for this is to practice.

Exercise
Perform a series of downhill reps but instead of finishing at the bottom of the hill
extend the rep by upto 200/300 metres beyond the end of the hill. Maintain the effort

down the hill and along the flat to the end of the rep. Treat the number of reps and the recovery as you would a normal hill rep.

From downhill to uphill

Even more of a shock to the system than the switch from downhill to level running is when you reach the bottom of the hill and have to start immediately climbing uphill again. This usually happens when you are crossing small valleys, down one side, cross a small stream and straight back up the other side with no real flat area at the bottom. Normally in these situations both the descent and the climb are quite steep as shallow sided valleys tend to have an extended valley floor.

In most cases this sudden change in movement pattern tends to make the runner resort to walking up the hill. This is partially due to the physical aspect of suddenly changing the work rate and the movement patterns of the muscles in the legs but also the physiological effect of the sudden change from relatively easy work downhill to a hard uphill effort. Yet again, the only way to really prepare for this is to practice.

Exercise

Perform a series of reps in a steep sided valley where you can run down and then straight back up again. The distance of the reps, including both down and up sections, should be between 600 to 800 metres.

Run down and then up. At the end of the rep take a recovery before repeating the rep in reverse to get back to your starting point. This would be classed as two reps. Perform a series of 10 to 12 reps.

The recovery should be between 50% to 100% of your running time dependant upon fitness.

If you have to walk the uphill, then still do the reps. The session is designed to replicate actual race conditions and to condition the body for the change from going down to going up.

3.1.10 Running with a rucksack

There are some disciplines in off-road running that require the carrying of a rucksack such as in a mountain marathon. In addition to this, a growing number of trail and fell runners are now carrying hydration sacks for long-distance events.

When running downhill with a sack on the back, the runner needs to be aware that this extra load can alter their centre of gravity and so may have an effect on the descending style and technique.

Obviously the smaller, more lightweight and closer to the body that the rucksack fits, the less of an effort that it will have. If the style and technique is affected then the angle of lean will be reduced and a more upright posture adopted. Similarly stride-length will also shorten especially on the shallower slopes where the runner may be accustomed to striding out.

One other aspect that will become apparent is that with the extra weight and bulk on the back, it can become more difficult to recover from a bad foot plant. This itself can lead to the runner becoming more cautious when descending at speed.

Running with a rucksack can alter the running style. Choosing smaller, lightweight sacks that fit close to the body can reduce the effects and allow a more natural style.

3.1.11 Footwear

When it comes to running downhill, shoes are an important part of the equation. The essence of successful down hilling is control although it may not often look that way. Therefore grip or possibly even more importantly, confidence in the gripping power of your shoes is essential. Even just the thought of slipping or falling can result in a loss in concentration and a poorer performance.

Nowadays shoes for off-road running are relatively easy to obtain with most manufacturers producing and most retailers stocking some form of off-road running shoe. As with all shoes there are differences between manufacturers and models and we could waffle on for hours about shoe construction.

That's not the purpose of this guide and so I'll keep it short. Basically off-road shoes breakdown into three types, the trail running shoe style with the relatively thick midsole, the fell running/orienteering shoe with the relatively thin midsole and the cross-country spike.

All three have their place in off-road running and each style has its own merits. The trail shoe style provides more support and cushioning and on routes that involve hard trail such as hard packed tracks and forest roads will provide more comfort to the runner.

By contrast, fell running/orienteering style shoes have very little in the line of a midsole. So when running on a hard surface you do tend to find that you feel every little stone and pebble. However, where they do come into their own is where the route is running over soft and rough terrain. Their thin midsole means that the foot is nearer to the ground so that on uneven surfaces the chances of turning the ankle or sustaining an injury are substantially reduced. Also their sole pattern tends to resemble a form of stud and on soft ground can provide exceptional grip.

The cross-country spike tends to be used purely as a racing shoe in XC events although some runners do use fell shoes instead.

Whether shoe style you use it is important to ensure that the tread, studs or spikes are not worn away or damaged. There is not much point in having them if they are no use. If they are worn then replace the sole or replace the shoe.

3.2 Mental attitude

The mind tends to have a very good sense of self-protection and quite often wouldn't let the body do what it considers to be unnatural and dangerous. As you will have noticed a lot of the techniques for effective running downhill involve moments that don't come naturally such as leaning into the slope or looking ahead of where your feet are placed. The mind therefore tends to lead a general reluctance to performing these actions.

The only way round this is to build up the confidence in your own ability to descend so that you are both familiar and comfortable with it, and to build up this confidence you need to practice, practice and practice again. Spend as much time in the hills as possible running downhill.

If you are fairly new to downhill running it may be advisable to start with shallow slopes, which are soft and grassy underfoot. If you do fall on these you will tend to bounce !

Falling and a possible injury in the early stages of progression will not help establish confidence in your own ability, and it cannot be stressed enough how much self-confidence plays in the ability to run well downhill.

As your confidence grows, slowly build up to steeper slopes with rougher terrain and longer descents. Like all things relating to structured training, it is a steady progression that is important. Persevere and in time, it will produce a startling change in your downhill ability.

4. Training Sessions for Improvement

4.1 Constructing a downhill session

It doesn't take a great deal of imagination to construct a session to improve your downhill techniques but you'll be surprised at how many runners never even contemplate it. Instead they'll just do their downhill training as and when they are running a descent on their long runs.

This is fine and it does work. After all, any downhill running is better than none but there is no doubt that including specific downhill sessions into your training will improve your abilities faster and more significantly.

Sessions can be based on

1. Downhill reps - similar to normal hill reps except that the effort is put into the running down instead of the running up. Difficult to think of having an uphill recovery but this can be taken as an easy jog or a walk. These can be done as reps of an equal distance or as a pyramid session.

2. Up and downhill reps - this is another variation on normal hill reps but instead of taking a recovery on the way down, the effort is continued on the downhill after the climb. The recovery being taken as a rest before starting the next uphill.
This form of session is particularly useful if training for a shortish straight up and down race as it gets the body accustomed to a hard effort coming down immediately after the hard climb. It will also help to develop pacing judgment for such events.

3. Structured fartlek. A structured fartlek session with an odd number of legs that comprise uphill, downhill and level running will train all aspects of your running. Treating the first leg as effort, the next as recovery and then the following as effort once again. If it's a three- leg fartlek then the first leg will then become the next recovery, etc. etc,

---

A pyramid session is a series of reps of varying distance typically along the lines of 200 metres, 300 metres, 400 metres. The idea is to run the 200 metres with effort, recover back to the start, run the 300 metres with effort, recover back to the start, run the 400 metres with effort, recover back to the start, run the 300 metres with effort, recover back to the start, run the 200 metres with effort, recover back to the start and then go back up the scale again.

They are a standard session for track and road runners but can easily be adapted by the off-road runner by performing them in more rugged terrain especially as uphill and downhill sessions.

4.1.1 Distances

As with uphill reps, a variety of distances can and should be used with downhill reps.

Short hills of between 30 and 60 seconds running time can be used to develop the use of technique and style. The short length means that a particular attribute such as holding the arms out for balance can be practiced, without the session being that long that concentration begins to waver. Many repetitions of short duration will help ingrain the correct running style into the body's movement pattern.

One other use of short hills is to help develop eccentric muscle strength. For short distances it is possible to really attack the descent and power your way down. It would be recommended to only do this session on a shallow descent with a good soft running surface such as grass.

For a skills session, the emphasis should be on practicing technique rather than running fast. A typical session would normally be between 20 to 30 descents broken down into 2 or 3 sets with a short recovery in between. This helps prevent concentration fatigue. For the more power based session, this would normally entail 3 sets of 8 reps with an easy jog/walk back up as the recovery between reps and a 5 to 7 minute easy recovery run between sets.

Medium hills of between 2 to 5 minutes will help aerobic capacity. A number of different sessions of this length representing different running surfaces and angles of descent should be built up. Normally sessions of this type will comprise of between 10 to 15 reps with an easy jog/walk back as the recovery.

One aspect that should not be overlooked is pushing the effort on to the flat beyond the end of the downhill. Most races don't end at the bottom of a hill but rather a distance away. This will help condition the body to the sudden change from running with a gravity assisted descent to more self-powered level running.

Long hills of over 5 minutes can be used to develop the body's ability to maintain pace and concentration. Hills with a descent time of longer than 5 minutes will be encountered in races. Therefore it should be no surprise that you should prepare for them.

Being practical the number of reps will depend upon the length of the hill. You can't say do 10 reps if the total time of going up and coming back down for each rep is going to be 30 minutes. The more logical way of looking at this is to keep the session to 60 minutes excluding warm-up and warm-down. Do as many reps as will fit into the 60 minutes.

Rolling hills can be incorporated into a long and/or steady run. Plan the route carefully to take in hills of a similar type that you want to train on and treat the descents as you would in a downhill session.

One element that must be factored into your descending sessions is the terrain. It would be advisable to build up a portfolio of different downhill sessions that would include hills of various angles of descent and different types of running surface ranging from smooth forest road to steep heather moor to loose scree. During a general training phase these sessions can be done on a rotational basis to build-up overall skill and conditioning. When training moves into a more specific phase geared to a particular race, the emphasis should move towards those downhill sessions that mirror the descents that would be encountered in the race.

After all if your target rate has some long steep rocky descents then practicing your downhill techniques on boggy moorland paths will not condition you to the descents that you will actually encounter.

4.1.2 So which type of sessions are suitable for which type of off-road running

The table overleaf details the various off-road disciplines and the relevant downhill sessions that are appropriate.

Event	Normal Length of Descent	Descent	Appropriate Type of Downhill Session
Cross-Country	Upto 400 metres. Rarely longer.	Upto 300 ft / 90 metres in one descent.	Short hills and Medium hills upto 3 minutes running time either as reps or fartlek.
Orienteering	Upto 1,000 metres. Rarely longer.	Upto 600 ft / 180 metres in one descent	Short hills and Medium hills either as reps or fartlek.
Short Trail Races (upto 10 miles/16 kms)	Upto 1 mile/1.5 km and there may be more than one descent.	Upto 1000 ft / 300 metres in one descent	Short hills and Medium hills either as reps or fartlek. Long hills as reps. Rolling hills as part of a weekend long run of upto 15 miles / 24 kms.
Short Fell Races (upto 6 miles/10 kms)	Upto 3 miles/5 kms. Normally only one descent but may be more.	Upto 2000 ft / 600 metres in one descent	Short hills and Medium hills either as reps or fartlek. Long hills as reps. Rolling hills as part of a weekend long run of upto 10 miles / 16 kms.
Medium and Long Trail Races (over 10 miles/16 kms)	Upto 2 miles/3 kms and there may be more than one descent.	Upto 1000 ft / 300 metres in one descent but some may go upto 2000 ft / 600 metres.	Short hills and Medium hills either as reps or fartlek. Long hills as reps. Rolling hills as part of a weekend long run of upto 20 miles / 32 kms.

Event	Normal Length of Descent	Descent	Appropriate Type of Downhill Session
Medium Fell Races (6 to 12 miles / 10 to 19 kms)	Upto 4 miles / 6.4 kms and there may be more than one descent.	Upto 4000 ft / 1200 metres in one descent.	Short hills and Medium hills either as reps or fartlek. Long hills as reps. Rolling hills as part of a weekend long run of upto 15 miles / 24 kms.
Long Fell Races (over 12 miles / 19 kms)	Upto 4 miles /6.4 kms and there will be more than one descent.	Upto 4000 ft / 1200 metres in one descent.	Short hills and Medium hills either as reps or fartlek. Long hills as reps. Rolling hills as part of a weekend long run of upto 20 + miles / 32 + kms.
Mountain Marathons	Upto 4 miles /6.4 kms and there will be more than one descent.	Upto 4000 ft / 1200 metres in one descent.	Medium hills as reps or fartlek. Long hills as reps. Rolling hills as part of a weekend long run of upto 20 + miles / 32 kms including carrying a ruck-sack.

4.1.3 How often should you do a downhill specific session?

Ideally once a week but being practical that would be difficult for a normal time-constrained runner to do. There are just too many other training aspects to consider. The best compromise solution would probably be to use a four week macrocycle with one week incorporating a downhill rep session, the following week an uphill rep session, the third week either a structured fartlek or up and downhill session and the fourth week a terrain training session. The terrain training would tend to include some element of up and down work. On the basis of two quality sessions per week this structure will provide for a regular hill session either up or down or both and still leave a slot for a weekly speed session.

With a weekend long run on the hill incorporating rolling hills, this should adequately prepare you for most things that will be thrown your way.

Therefore the macro training plan for a four week cycle would look like this.

	Week 1	**Week 2**	**Week 3**	**Week 4**
Quality Session 1 Hill session	Downhill reps	Uphill reps	Structured fartlek or a Up & Down session	Terrain training
Quality Session 2 Speed session	Speed	Speed	Speed	Speed
Weekend Run	Long run including rolling hills	Long run including rolling hills	Long run including rolling hills	Long run including rolling hills

A macrocycle is a training plan over an extended period of time such as shown for a month or four week cycle. A microcycle is a shorter training period which would normally detail seven days or one week.

4.2 Putting it all together.

All the different aspects of running downhill from conditioning the body to the various technique tricks of the trade have been explored.

In this last section we will look at four specific scenarios and putting all the techniques together, see how they look. The four scenarios are :

1. Shallow descent, good running surface.
2. Medium descent, , medium surface.
3. Steep descent, rough surface.
4. Steep descent, scree surface.

One final tip.

It is always a good idea to watch the downhill style of other runners, particularly those who are better descenders then yourself. If you get the opportunity even follow them downhill, just a few strides behind and try to place your feet where theirs have been.

Now get out there and practice !

One way to watch yourself descending is to get somebody to film your descents during training with a camcorder. Watching how you descend will enable you to spot areas in your technique that can be improved. Then go back and practice .....

4.2.1 Shallow descent, good running surface.

On a shallow descent with a good running surface it is possible to maintain a normal running action.

Stride length can be normal and it may even be possible to slightly over-stride and gain extra distance per each stride.

There is no need to use the arms for additional balance and they should follow the normal endurance runner's techniques of close to the side and moving backwards and forwards, slightly crossing the body.

Eyes should still be focussed three to eight paces in front to assess the ground, ahead.

The maximum benefit can be obtained from the angle of lean by leaning forward from the waist without any undue worry of loss of stability. Normal foot plant can be maintained whether it is toe first or heel first.

Be aware that adverse weather conditions such as mud , snow, or ice etc may mean that these techniques may have to be modified.

4.2.2 Medium descent, medium surface.

Here the angle of descent is steeper and the surface may be grass, track or path.
Stride length will be slightly shortened due to the increased angle of descent.
This is on the border line as to whether the arms are used to aid balance or used in
the normal running style.
The eyes are still focussed ahead assessing the ground.
The angle of lean can still be used to benefit momentum and control the speed of
descending.
The foot should be planted in the plantar flexed position with the full sole making
contact with the ground.

4.2.3 Steep descent, rough surface.

The angle of descent is steep and the surface may be grass, heather, rock, earth or any combination.

The stride length is drastically reduced. In the worst case scenario it can resemble walking downstairs. With the more fit and nimble it is possible to do a semi-bound or leap down sections of the descent.

Both the steep descent and the rough surface make the downhill unstable so use the outstretched arms as a balance aid as much as possible.

Focus the eyes three to four steps in front of you. It is particularly important on steep rough descents due to the unstable nature of the ground and the need to spot potential hazards.

The angle of lean is more upright, closer to the vertical. Leaning too far forward will make the runner too top heavy.

The foot should be planted with the full sole making contact with the ground.

4.2.4 Steep descent, scree surface.

The angle of descent is steep and the surface is scree or loose stone varying in size from little glass marbles to dinner plates.

Stride length is drastically reduced. In the worst case scenario it can resemble walking downstairs.

Both the steep descent and the rough surface make the downhill unstable so use the outstretched arms as much as possible.

Focus the eyes three to four steps in front of you. It is particularly important on steep rough descents due to the unstable nature of the surface.

Keep the body vertical but relaxed.

Don't plant the foot flat, instead land with the heels first and dig them into the scree. Let the body slide a little so that the heels dig further in.

5. Summary

As runners we are all seeking improvement. Even if we are not competing at the sharp end of the field we are still in competition, normally with ourselves, to beat that best time.

For the off-road runner, running well downhill is a crucial factor in your overall running performance. Follow the techniques and training suggestions in this guide and you will see your times come down (forgive the pun !). Perhaps even more importantly they may just give you the edge over that other runner that you keep bumping into at races................

The author enjoying himself.

About the Author

Kev Shevels is a man who has forgotten more than most about off-road running. Its not that he knew it in the first place, its just that at his age the memory has started to go along with lots of other things such as a slim waistline ....

A runner for over thirty years, Kev has been involved in off-road running for over twenty-eight of those years. During this time he has tried his hand at most of the different styles of this discipline, from fell, to trail, to mountain marathons, to ultra-trails, to orienteering, to mountain running. During this time he managed to raise himself up from being a lousy-level runner all the way to the dizzy heights of mediocrity. However, what he did also do is pick up an extensive knowledge and experience of running off-road which he has been able to pass onto others through coaching and encouragement.

A founder member of the Quakers Running Club and Durham Fell Runners, two of the most enthusiastic off-road running clubs in the North East, Kev has been a qualified UK Athletics Level 3 coach for the past nine years, specialising in Fell and Hill Running. Most of his coaching nowadays being done through Durham Fell Runners and the Run Off-Road organisation.

However, to some people his main claim to fame is as a race organiser. Over the last ten years, Kev has organised numerous races, from fell, to trail, to road and cross-country. Some years even organising as many as twenty events which partially explains the lack of training and the fact that he can no longer see his toes.

When not running, coaching or just promoting off-road running, Kev is an active member of his local mountain rescue team.

Acknowledgements

For encouragement, support and not a little bit of humour ....

Lynne Shevels
Harry Manuel
Stu Ferguson
Gerry Hehir

And to all those runners who I have coached over the years and who allowed me to "experiment".

The Run Off-Road Series

Run Off-Road is the name adopted by Trailguides for it's publications aimed at the fell, hill, trail and mountain runner. This series of books is designed to promote the sport of off-road running in all it's many forms and to encourage the participants to improve and develop their abilities and skills in order to further increase their enjoyment of the sport.

This is an evolving series of books that is constantly expanding. See our website at www.trailguides.co.uk and subscribe to our newsletter for regular updates on our range of publications.

At the time of writing the titles in the series include:

An Introduction to Trail and Fell Running
Downhill Techniques for Off-Road Runners
Uphill Techniques for Off-road Runners
Terrain Training for Off-road Runners
Mountain Marathon Preparation
Navigation for Off-Road Runners
Long and Ultra Distance Off-Road Running

Disclaimer

The information contained in these pages is provided in good faith, but no warranty is made for its accuracy. The contents are, at the time of writing and to the best of my knowledge, up-to-date and correct. However, the world is a changing environment and what is correct one day may not be so the next. The suggested training regimes contained in this publication are exactly that, suggested. It is the reader's responsibility to judge their own level of fitness and whether they are capable of performing any of the said activities.

No guarantee whatsoever is provided by the author and his team and no liability is accepted for any loss, damage or injury of any kind resulting from the use of these pages. Nor as a result of any defect or inaccuracy in them.

As with all outdoor activities, you and you alone are responsible for your safety and well being.